Fun Chinese Characters 2
快乐汉字 2

Ping Xu Moroney

许平

ISBN:0990665623
ISBN-13: 978-0-9906656-2-5

DEDICATION

To my mom, husband and three children

Ping Xu Moroney 许平

CONTENTS

Most people think learning Chinese characters is difficult and hard. It can be. However, it is very rewarding as Chinese characters are the crystallization of the Chinese ancestors. Developed over five thousand years, it is one of the world's most ancient texts. The key to reading Chinese is in decoding the charm of Chinese characters as the image of the world lurks in a wealth of aesthetics and poetry. With practice you can learn to see the images embedded in the characters; when this happens, reading Chinese becomes fun and easy. This approach is suitable for students of all ages and nationalities. The watercolor paintings transfer the process of learning, boring and complex, into excitement and animation. This approach to learning allows more people to love and appreciate the unique magic of the ancient Chinese characters.

ACKNOWLEDGMENTS

I could not have completed the Fun Chinese Characters book two without Dr. Lan Jiang and Dr. Ming Jian of William Paterson University. I would like to express a special thanks to all the students and colleagues whom I was fortunate to work with at the Mountain View Middle School in NJ and Orange County Chinese Language School in NY. Lisa Djonbalic, Director of Elite Kids International & World Languages Coordinator.

CHAPTER 1 数字 SHÙ ZÌ NUMBER

1. 百 bǎi hundred
2. 零 líng zero
3. 万 wàn ten thousand
4. 千 qiān thousand

1 百 bǎi
hundred

2 零 líng
zero

3 千 qiān
thousand

4 万 wàn
ten thousand

5. 忡 chōng sad
6. 淡 dàn light
7. 叨 dāo grumble
8. 古 gǔ old
9. 老 lǎo aged
10. 杰 jié her
11. 旧 jiù old
12. 利 lì sharp
13. 美 měi beauty
14. 坦 **tǎn** flat
15. 鲜 xiān fresh
16. 闲 xián idl
17. 香 xiāng fragant
18. 忠 zhōng faithful
19. 仲 zhòng intermediary
20. 坝 bà dam

5 忡 chōng
sad

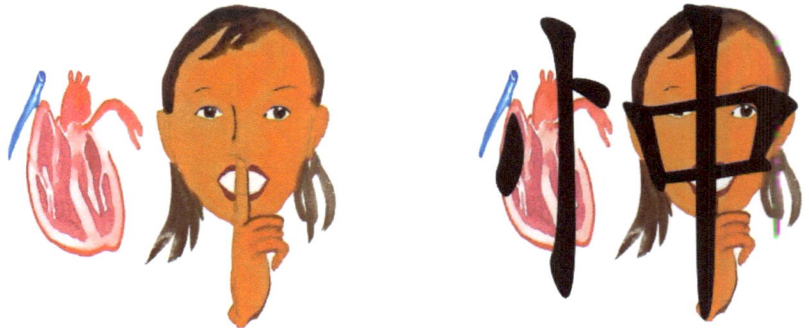

6 淡 dàn
light

7 叨 dāo
grumble

8 古 gǔ
old

9 老 lǎo
aged

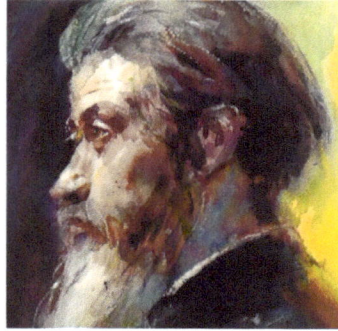

10 杰 jié
hero

11 旧 jiù
old

12 利 lì
sharp

13 美 měi
beauty

14 坦 tǎn
flat

15 鲜 xiān
fresh

16 闲 xián
idle

美
坦
鲜
闲

17 香 xiāng
fragant

18 忠 zhōng
faithful

19 仲 zhòng
intermediary

20 坝 bà
dam

CHAPTER 3 名词 MÍNG CÍ NOUN

21. 冰 bīng ice
22. 尘 chén dirt
23. 仇 chóu enemy
24. 胆 dǎn gut
25. 肚 dǔ belly
26. 恩 ēn kindness
27. 副 fù deputy
28. 羔 gāo young
29. 宫 gōng palace
30. 果 guǒ fruit
31. 海 hǎi ocean
32. 季 jì season
33. 间 jiān between
34. 件 jiàn item
35. 雷 léi thunder
36. 泪 lèi tear
37. 类 lèi kind
38. 里 lǐ inside
39. 李 lǐ plum
40. 杩 mǎ headboard
41. 苗 miáo seedling
42. 梅 méi plum flower
43. 闷 mèn melancholy

8

44. 萌 méng sprout
45. 仁 rén benevolence
46. 山 shān mountain
47. 闪 shǎn flash
48. 闩 shuān bolt
49. 孙 sūn grandchild
50. 体 tī body
51. 天 tiān sky
52. 土 tǔ earth
53. 仙 xiān god
54. 相 hǎi ocean
55. 芯 xìn core
56. 信 xìn letter
57. 杏 xìng apricot
58. 烟 yān smoke
59. 样 yàng style
60. 洋 yáng ocean
61. 叶 yè leaf
62. 婴 yīng baby
63. 员 yuán member
64. 箱 xiāng box

21 冰 bīng
ice

22 尘 chén
dirt

23 仇 chóu
enemy

24 胆 dǎn
gut

25 肚 dǔ
belly

26 恩 ēn
kindness

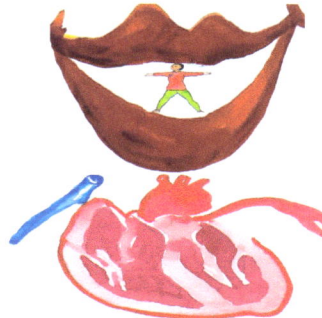

27 副 fù
deputy

28 羔 gāo
young

29 宫 gōng

palace

30 果 guǒ

fruit

31 海 hǎi

ocean

32 季 jì

season

33 间 jiān
between

34 件 jiàn
item

35 雷 léi
thunder

36 泪 lèi
tear

37 类 lèi
kind

38 里 lǐ
inside

39 李 lǐ
plum

40 杩 mǎ
headboard

41 苗 miáo
seedling

42 梅 méi
plum flower

43 闷 mèn
melancholy

44 萌 méng
sprout

45 仁 rén
benevolence

46 山 shān
mountain

47 闪 shǎn
flash

48 闩 shuān
bolt

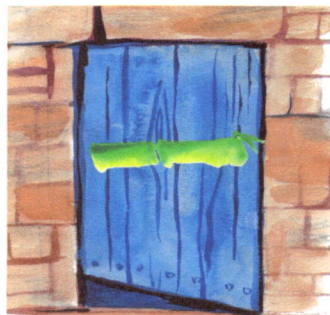

49 孙 sūn
grandchild

50 体 tī
body

51 天 tiān
sky

52 土 tǔ
earth

53 仙 xiān
god

54 相 xiāng
photo

55 芯 xìn
core

56 信 xìn
letter

57 杏 xìng
apricot

58 烟 yān
smoke

59 样 yàng
style

60 洋 yáng
ocean

61 叶 yè
leaf

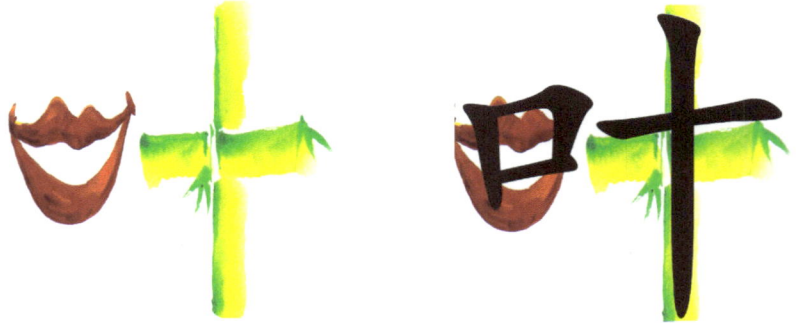

62 婴 yīng
baby

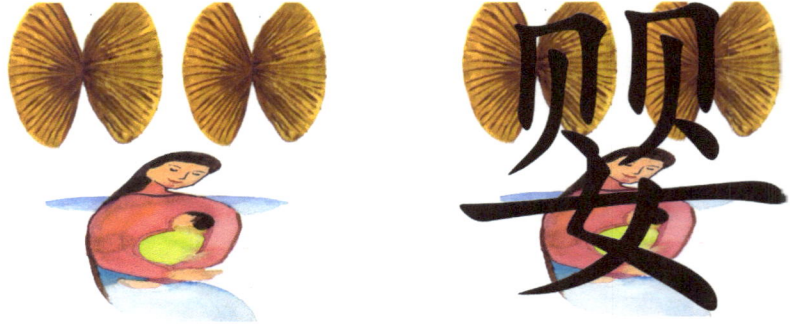

63 员 yuán
member

64 箱 xiāng
box

CHAPTER4 动词 DÒNG CÍ VERB

65. 崩 bēng collapse
66. 呗 bei chant
67. 查 chá check
68. 唱 chàng sing
69. 出 chū go out
70. 冲 chōng clash
71. 倡 chàng initiate
72. 闯 chuǎng rush
73. 赐 cì grant
74. 呆 dāi stay
75. 分 fēn divide
76. 吓 hè scare
77. 回 huí circle
78. 会 huì meet
79. 间 jiān room
80. 骂 mà insult
81. 冒 mào risk
82. 描 miáo trace
83. 问 wèn ask
84. 闻 wén hear
85. 扪 mén touch
86. 焖 mèn stew
87. 瞄 miáo aim
88. 鸣 míng chirp

89. 思 sī think

90. 谈 tán talk

91. 吐 tǔ spit

92. 想 xiǎng think

93. 休 xiū rest

94. 照 zhào reflect

95. 召 lǐ summon

96. 种 zhǒng grow

65 崩 bēng
collapse

66 呗 bei
chant

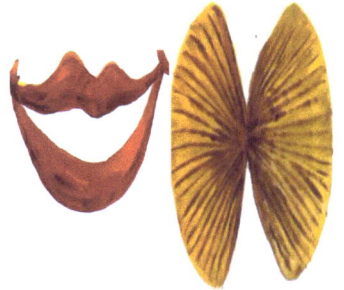

67 查 chá
check

68 唱 chàng
sing

69 出 chū
go out

70 冲 chōng
clash

71 倡 chàng
initiate

72 闯 chuǎng
rush

73 赐 cì
grant

74 呆 dāi
stay

75 分 fēn
divide

76 吓 hè
scare

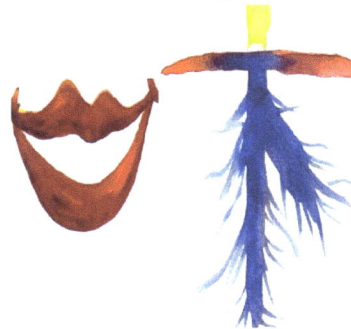

77 回 huí
circle

78 会 huì
meet

79 间 jiān
room

80 骂 mà
insult

81 冒 mào
risk

82 描 miáo
trace

83 问 wèn
ask

84 闻 wén
hear

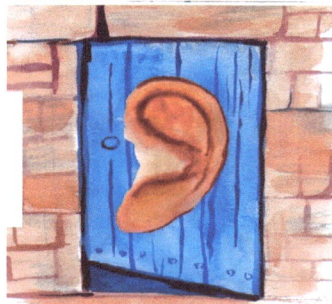 

85 扪 mén
touch

86 焖 mèn
stew

87 瞄 miáo
aim

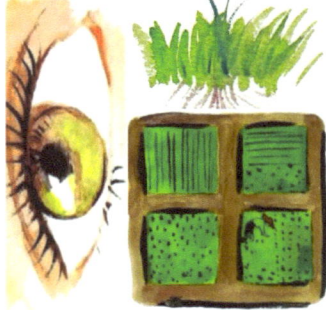

88 鸣 míng
chirp

89 思 sī
think

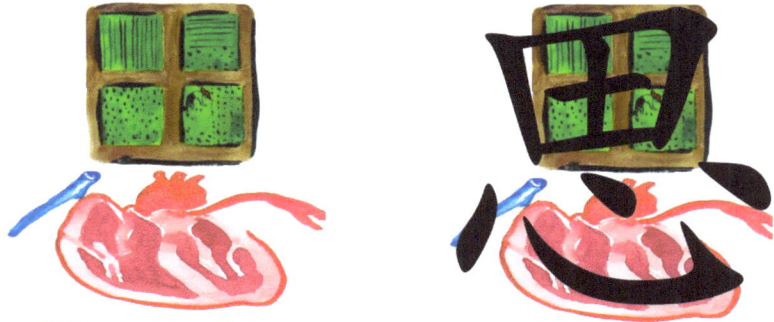

90 谈 tán
talk

91 吐 tǔ
spit

92 想 xiǎng
think

93 休 xiū
rest

94 照 zhào
reflect

95 召 zhào
summon

96 种 zhǒng
grow

CHAPTER 5 连词　LIÁN CÍ　CONJUNCTION

97.肿 **zhǒng** swollen

98.但 dàn but

99.和 hé and

100.因 yīn because

97 肿 zhǒng
swollen

98 但 dàn
but

99 和 hé
and

100 因 yīn
because

ABOUT THE AUTHOR

许平 Ping Xu Moroney
www.pingsgallery.com
pingsgallery@aol.com

Ping Xu Moroney was born and studied Chinese art in Shanghai China. She holds a Bachelor's degree in secondary education from Shanghai Teachers Advanced College, a bachelor's degree in International Studies from Kyoritsu Women's University in Japan, a Master's degree in Studio Arts from The College of New Rochelle, and a teaching certificate in Chinese from William Paterson University. She has experience teaching art, Chinese, Japanese and Asian culture subjects in private and public schools in NJ and NY. As a professional artist, she has exhibited and sold fine art paintings through art dealers, galleries and art exhibits in China, Japan and America.

许平出生在上海，自幼学中国画，上海第四师范学校毕业后留学日本。1999 年获日本共立女子大学国际关系学士学位。后移居美国，2003 年获新罗谢尔学院硕士学位。她的作品在当地市政厅，公共图书馆和其他博物馆多有展示和收藏。2010 年学完威廉帕特森大学"汉语教师培养项目"，现已获得新泽西州终身汉语和美术教师资格证书。她已有多年在纽约和新泽西州公立和私立的学校教学经验。

www.ingramcontent.com/pod-product-compliance
Lightning Source LLC
Chambersburg PA
CBHW041526070426

42452CB00036B/28